MEL BAY PRESENTS
European flavor
BY JAMES FAZIO

14 ACCORDION SOLOS ON EUROPEAN MELODIES

Table of Contents

1 2 3 4 5 6 7 8 9 0

Visit us on the Web at www.melbay.com — E-mail us at email@melbay.com

Foreword

The past three consecutive summers have been a delightful and rare opportunity for my family and me. Having friends in Germany, we where able to stay free and tour much of Europe, visiting France, Switzerland, Austria, Italy, and most of Germany. Our place of residence was in a beautiful home in a little town called Muhlhausen. Located in the residential village is a wonderful German restaurant where we had dinner one evening. When I asked "Wo ist die akkordeon spiele?" (Where is the accordion player?), the woman and owner replied in German, "We do not have one, but we do own an accordion." She asked if I knew how to play, and for two hours after dinner I entertained about forty Germans while strolling through this beautiful restaurant. She was so delighted she gave me a bottle of the house wine, and treated all of us to a wonderful homemade dessert, and a hug. She also asked if I could return and play again, and two weeks later I did, having already written "A Little Town Called Muhlhausen" in her honor. She loved it!

All of the other songs are about places we have seen or done. "Cittadella" is about a small, quaint walled city in Northern Italy (Tuscany) where we spent a night. As we walked from our hotel through the small streets, the melody of this song was in my head, but not yet on paper. We had stumbled into an Italian Pizza Parlor, and we were hungry!

I hope you enjoy the sounds of European Flavor and vicariously travel down the Rhine River to Bingen and Rudesheim, two of the many beautiful towns along the rhine and my inspiration for (*A Trip on the Rhine*), or stay overnight some 15,000 feet in the Austrian Alps in Brandt, Austria (*Alpine Dream*). You might dance your way through a medieval Festival in Innsbrook, Austria (*Tyrolean Dance #1*).

Each song has its own story to tell, But can best be appreciated by playing and enjoying the sounds of *European Flavor*.

About the Author

Inspired by Myron Floren on the Lawrence Welk Show, I began playing the accordion at the age of six and distinctly remember my father enforcing my half hour practice sessions because the lessons cost $2.50 a week. My studies continued throughout my high school education. Playing my way through college, I graduated with a B.S. in Secondary Education/ Earth Space Science in 1976 from the University of Pittsburgh. Currently a science teacher, I continue to be an active accordionist playing for many exclusive private and public functions, as well as entertaining the elderly in assisted living homes. I have always enjoyed writing and playing originals and am currently working on another collection based upon a recent trip to Europe. I would like to dedicate this book to my lovely wife Gretchen and my boys Jimmy and Christopher, who put up with many hours of playing each day.

A Little Town Called Mühlhausen

by James C. Fazio

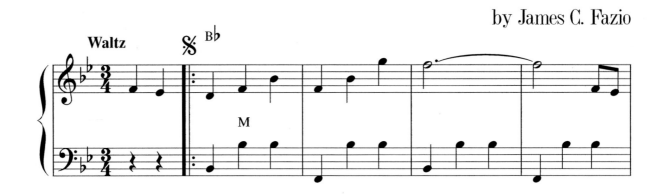

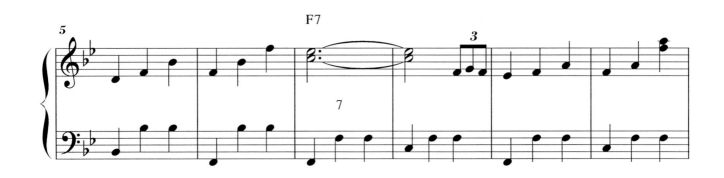

Le Café Paris

by James C. Fazio

Tango Del Vino

by James C. Fazio

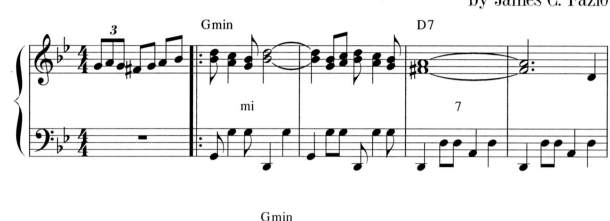

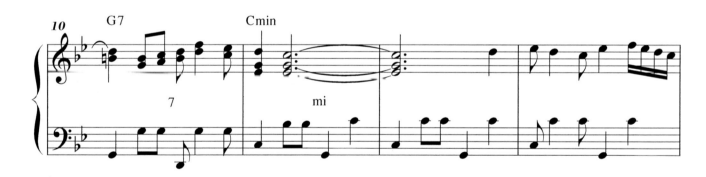

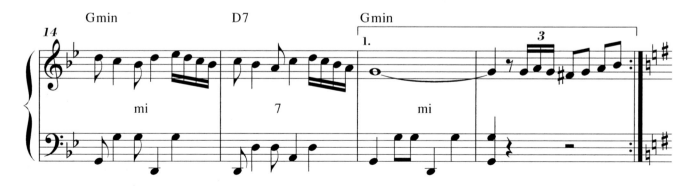

Bavarian March

by James C. Fazio

Italian Festival

Lightly, with spirit

by James C. Fazio

My Love

by James C. Fazio

Eine Reise Auf Die Rhine
(A Trip On The Rhine)

by James C. Fazio

Cittadella

by James C. Fazio

Venezia

by James C. Fazio

Alpine Dream

by James C. Fazio

Tarantella Tuscano

by James C. Fazio

35

Italian Love Affair

by James C. Fazio

Tyrolean Dance

by James C. Fazio

With spirit, not too fast

The Italian Vineyards

by James C. Fazio